Je

An Inward Journey
Through Lent

Marilyn Gustin

Imprimi Potest:
Thomas D. Picton, C.Ss.R.
Provincial, Denver Province
The Redemptorists

ISBN 978-0-7648-1571-3

Printed in the United States of America
07 08 09 10 11 5 4 3 2 1

Liguori Publications, a nonprofit corporation, is an apostolate of the Redemptorists. To learn more about the Redemptorists, visit Redemptorists.com.

To order, call 1-800-325-9521
www.liguori.org

Introduction

It's an indelible image from one Easter morning. The rising sun? No. A cross now glorious with flowers? No. What then? Well, it was Betty, hugging the—but I'm ahead of my story.

Betty announced to her friends at the beginning of that Lent that she was giving up coffee for the season. We were astounded. It was hard to imagine Betty without a coffee cup in her hand. But she was determined to do something "significant," as she put it, for her Lenten discipline. So we applauded her goal. And week after week we encouraged her, cheered for her, commiserated with her. With all that support, how could she not succeed? And she did. No coffee—all through Lent.

Then came the Easter Vigil at our retreat house, where it was fully celebrated in the ancient, magnificent way. We began at 10:00 PM on Holy Saturday and finished about 1:00 on

Easter morning. Feeling exalted and happy, we made our way to the dining room—but Betty got there first. She headed straight for the coffee machine. She took a full pot to a table and there she sat, her arms around it, draining cup after cup until the pot was empty.

Even today, I see her there. I still ask, how significant was her Lenten exercise? What good did all her discipline do? Did she transform herself? Did she get rid of an exaggerated habit? Did she loosen an attachment? Was she any closer to God? She *was* happier in that moment, but it seemed to have a lot more to do with coffee than with Easter or her own spiritual life.

Is this what Lent is for—to make us relatively miserable for all those weeks so we can feel relief on Easter morning? Too many of us, for too long, have tried this.

Lent is really a joyful season, because it looks forward to the Easter experience of spiritual transformation—transformation that makes our living richer, more joyful, filled with love and serenity. Lent will create those conditions in our hearts and our lives if we cooperate with the process. Then Easter becomes an expression of our own spiritual resurrection as well as a celebration of the resurrection of Jesus.

Lent is for transforming ourselves—and not because we are bad people. We're generally not. We need transformation because we experience ourselves as separate from God, separate from others, maybe even separate from ourselves. We feel that our identity ends with our skin. In truth, we are much bigger, much more, because the Holy Spirit lives inside us and expresses itself through us.

So the first purpose of Lent is to let our hearts be as enlivened as possible—opening and being revitalized. God is waiting with love for us to say yes to the grace of Lent. Our "yes" is most powerful when it is the root of action. We can cooperate with God's transformative love for us. If you work with this pamphlet during Lent, you will explore ways to enliven your heart—and to let God transform it even further.

Another magnificent spiritual use for Lent: to empower our will. This is perhaps a little closer to what we've always thought. However, the will has a deeper purpose than helping us behave well. The Christian mystics have known that the will is central to living in love and joy, so they emphasized practices that would empower that central aspect of ourselves.

Have you ever gone on a retreat or to a spiritual conference? Remember how you came home feeling marvelous, loving God, full of resolutions for a deeper spiritual life? Didn't you feel as if God had given you great gifts that you wanted to integrate and experience always? It was wonderful, that spiritual high!

Three weeks later, how was it? You remember, I remember. The trouble is, we leak. We are like sieves for the Spirit. It's not that our spiritual experience wasn't real—it was more real than much of our daily life. We felt different later because we were not strong enough inside to hold all that spiritual power. To contain our experience of the Spirit, we must become inwardly strong and solid. Such inner strength is primarily the power of will.

So to cooperate with our transformation into more love and joy and more experience of God, we can follow a double track this Lent: the enlivening of our heart and the empowering of our will.

I recommend that you read through this pamphlet quickly to get an idea where we're going. Then begin with Ash Wednesday and live each week as suggested. This is different from taking one exercise for all of Lent, but it will enrich your life. To accompany these practices, keeping a journal will help a lot.

Let's begin.

Ash Wednesday

"Remember that you are dust and to dust you will return." These words are said by the priest as he makes the sign of the cross in ashes on our foreheads. Why this reminder about dying?

It's useful, from a spiritual viewpoint, to recall often that our lives are fleeting, that our daily choices matter, and that living is a treasure. There is poignance in remembering that life passes swiftly, but there is joy in it too, because everything becomes so precious.

If we let go of our cultural resistance to thinking about death, we will find that its poignance is heart-opening. I recall one spring in Vermont when I'd been meditating on death. I recalled how everything that lives also dies—every plant, every animal, and every human being. I felt a certain sweetness as I drove one day, because I could almost taste the passing of it all. Suddenly one young tree—the freshest, greenest in the woods—jumped into my perception. My heart leapt, this lovely thing was so precious, so exquisite. Then my heart "got it." It wasn't only this one beautiful tree that was so precious—every tree in the woods, every blade of grass, every young vine and budding flower, every passing cloud—and even myself—we are all so very precious!

That is what Ash Wednesday really asks us to remember: how precious each moment of our living is, how beautiful every expression of Spirit in life is. The heart knows the beauty and the value of everything, large or small. It loves them all. The heart also holds our soul, our essence, which does not die, but lives on.

So, in the days after Ash Wednesday, you may wish to relax for a few minutes and ponder how magnificent and how fleeting life is on this earth. When you wash the ashes from your forehead, remember their message and offer appreciation to God for the life you've been given and the beauty it expresses. This will begin to awaken your heart. Your Lenten adventure has begun.

FIRST WEEK OF LENT

Beginning the Transformation

Suggested Scripture Readings

Besides the story of Jesus' last days on earth, you may enjoy these: 1 John 3:1–3; 1 Corinthians 13:4–7 (This will be familiar, but remember to read as if it were new to you.); Psalm 103:1–5

Reflection

One of the most time-honored ways the Church offers to enliven our hearts during Lent is to reflect deeply on Jesus' suffering and death. This phase of Jesus' life has been the spiritual mainstay for some of our most beloved saints, like Francis and Teresa of Avila. It was vital to them—and can be vital to us—because they recognized the greatest expression of Jesus' love for all humankind in his willingness to suffer and die.

When we are privileged to see someone take on a great challenge for someone else's sake, isn't it inspiring? Doesn't our heart warm with appreciation, admiration, and even love? It's why we cherish the stories of heroism, stories of great rescues, stories of risk-taking, stories of the long-term dedication of parents who adopt children with handicaps.

We've heard the detailed story of Jesus' suffering so often that we may not feel much any more. Frequently we think we should be sorrowful over his experience. But we cannot—and should not—conjure up something we don't feel. Rather, we can reflect on Jesus' experience by reading one of the gospel accounts (Luke 22:39—23:56 or Mark 14:32—15:47) as if we had never heard it before. For the moment, lay aside everything you think you know about it and read it for yourself. Imagine all this happening to someone you love.

Before you begin, pray that the living Christ

may help you open your heart—not to pain and sorrow but to love and gratitude.

You may want to do this every day this week. It's not a long story, but in the tradition of the great Christians who have lived before us, you may find your heart softening and expanding with love. Then this first week of Lent, though poignant indeed, may begin a transformation you will want to keep forever.

Practices for the Week

The most time-honored way to empower our will during Lent is to "do something hard." For many that has meant doing without something and this can have value if you know exactly what your purpose is—that is, not merely to endure. An athlete doesn't train hard only to make himself struggle. He trains hard so that by honing his will he can compete with more power, more effectiveness when the practice is over. So it is with us. If we choose to do something difficult, it is useless unless it will help us live with more love, pray with more power, and know God more intimately when Lent is over.

So if you wish to do something challenging this week, choose something meaningful. If you have a bad habit you'd like to let go of, doing without it is a good practice. (However, if you choose to create a new habit, remember that it requires three full weeks of repetition to establish any new habit.) Or you may wish to choose something that builds a new quality into your life, like trying to stay in the present moment more.

Choose so that on Easter Sunday you will have not only succeeded but made a noticeable change in your spiritual life.

Second Week of Lent

Contemplating Jesus' Life

Suggested Scripture Readings

In addition to those already mentioned, read Psalm 42:1–3; Psalm 19:14; Mark 14:32–38. (Where are you in this story?)

Reflection

Last week, you were encouraged to enliven your heart by reflecting on Jesus' passion and death. It's not the only way.

Another beautiful, heart-expanding reflection is on the life of Jesus. How did he live? What was he like? Why did people follow him in huge crowds? (Remember, theology about Jesus wasn't around yet!) Why have so many people over the centuries found him captivating, compelling?

When we concentrate only on the last few days of Jesus' life, we can easily get the feeling that Jesus was sad and solemn—making miracles, to be sure, but still a sorrowful person. This just cannot be how it was!

What kind of person do you like to be with? What kind of person would you run down the road after? What kind of person attracts you? I'll bet it's not somebody who's always as serious as a corpse.

Each of us will benefit from answering these questions for ourselves. The best way to discover Jesus anew is to encounter him in the gospel stories by reading them as if they are new to you. If you actually have not read them, so much the better for this exercise!

For this week, you may wish to leave the passion stories aside. You can begin by reading one of the gospels (preferably Mark or Luke) at one sitting. (They are shorter than you may think!) As you read, ask yourself questions like those above. Or you may wish to begin by pondering only a few stories. Here are some possibilities:

Imagine yourself in the front row of the crowd for the multiplication of the bread and fish (Matthew 14:13–21) or walking beside Jesus on the way to Jairus' house and he invites you to go inside with him (Luke 8:40–56). What might it have been like to have dinner with Jesus and his friends? (Luke 19:1–10). Why do you suppose his non-friends accused him of drinking too much? (Matthew 11:18–19). And while you're seeking to open your heart, don't ignore the baby Jesus (Matthew 2 or Luke 2—but you'll have to use your imagination).

Or you may wish to dip into the gospels at a random point and discover your own pleasure with it—see for yourself if you can find a picture of Jesus that touches your heart. Seek inside yourself, and yes, use your imagination, to find the Jesus you could like, the Jesus you'd want to hang out with. He surely was at least that attractive!

Practices for the Week

Discipline has a confused connotation for most of us. In general, we resist it and say things like, "I just don't have any self-discipline." So we think we are deficient in will power.

But that's not where the issue lies. We are not lacking in self-discipline, but rather, we do not have a deep enough desire.

Let's say you totally love being on a high mountain. It's not easy to climb those high ones, even with trails. But no one who loves the heights thinks it takes discipline to get there. Or maybe you like to play golf. Sometimes it's difficult, often frustrating. Sometimes it's great. Did it take discipline to bear all that? Of course not! You love it, so you just do it.

The reality is, many of us don't have much desire to be a full disciple of Jesus. We love him a little, maybe, and we honor him at a distance. Or we think we should love him. But to be a close comrade of Jesus, inside our own souls, how much desire do you have for that?

Be honest with yourself. It's an important question. If you don't have much desire for intimacy with Jesus, then you will believe that self-discipline is required to spend a lot of time in prayer, for example. Then, you say you lack discipline. You likely feel guilty besides.

This week, you may wish to reflect on how much desire you actually experience for intimacy with Jesus or for deep, inner discipleship. Do not be afraid of whatever you discover. You cannot change anything you don't see and feel, so be adventurous! Once you know clearly what you feel, there are further steps. We'll look at those next week.

THIRD WEEK OF LENT

Your Attitude on Gratitude

Suggested Scripture Readings

Philippians 4:6; Luke 17:12–17; Psalm 63:1–4; Psalm 107:1–9, 21

Reflection

One of the easiest and most beautiful heart enliveners is gratitude. One modern teacher has said, "If you know gratitude, you live in ecstasy." What a promise!

We often think of being grateful as only spontaneous. But it can also be intentional. That's when it brings splendid spiritual openness.

What has been your relationship to gratitude? Does it come easily to you? Do you find yourself constantly thanking everyone for what they do and what they are? Or do you take the good things for granted? Do you feel entitled to the kindness of your family or friends?

Feeling and expressing gratefulness, or expressing it first and then feeling it (which also counts!), helps us be more aware of how lovely our life is. It's so easy to get caught in wanting something more or something different. It's easy to fall into discontent and then we are indeed unhappy. But when we make a conscious effort to increase our thanksgiving and to praise God for everything in a day—well, I can only say, "try it—you'll enjoy it!"

When we practice gratitude, we cooperate with God's opening of our heart to him, to love, to life. We increase our saying "thank you" because it smoothes our relationships, it warms the feelings of those who receive our thanks, it pleases us and pleases others. Expressing thanks also helps us see more to appreciate.

So how can we practice gratitude? Here are some suggestions, but let your heart lead you:

- Keep a gratitude journal, listing five or ten things each evening that you are grateful for. Every evening's list must be new and different—that's the game, that's the practice.
- When you are with people, pay attention and find something to thank each one for, even if it's "thanks for all you do."
- Especially make a point of thanking your spouse and family for everything—doing the laundry, earning an income, mowing the lawn, cleaning the bathroom—all those daily things.
- Before you roll out of bed each morning, give thanks to God for waking up, for life, for the new day, for the beauty of those you share life with, for God's love that constantly enfolds and caresses you.

If you train your mind and heart to be grateful, there's always a bonus: more beauty, more love, more abundance flows to you without effort. It's a great adventure!

Practices for the Week

Last week you looked at the intensity of your desire for a living relationship with Christ. Let's say that you found a small desire that you'd like to increase. You may begin with prayer, something like this: "Lord, I don't feel much desire for you, but something in me wants to desire your friendship more. Please help me to want to want you!" Honest prayer is the best! It's always answered.

Now let's say maybe you're reluctant about Jesus Christ because you think of him as a judge, a high authority who's measuring you all the time. If that's what I thought of him, I wouldn't be interested in such a relationship either. You can try this: choose one moment from the stories about Jesus when he seemed like someone you'd like to know better. Perhaps when he was kind to someone, or when he called the children to him over his disciples' objections, or when he promised his followers that he would always be with them. Then imagine being with Jesus in that moment. What do you feel like? What do you appreciate about him? Is he tender with you? Kind? Loving? Happy? Spend as much time in this imagining as you wish—it is a wonderful form of prayer. By Saturday, do you feel a little more eager for the company of Christ?

Maybe you deeply want more desire for Christ. Here's one practice you might not expect: Thérèse of Lisieux (the Little Flower) once said, "The more content you are with your faults, the more lovely a garden is your heart for the Lord to roam in."

Surprised? We may feel we must attack our faults and get rid of them. But Saint Thérèse discovered that the very thoughts that condemn our faults also darken our heart. To experience the Lord's presence, we need to be more like him. Christ accepts us without a wisp of condemnation. He knows only love, nothing else. So we need to be patient with ourselves and not condemn our so-called faults, but focus on Christ instead. Then Christ can live in our hearts as he enjoys—and we can enjoy—his presence too.

To heighten your desire for a deep, intimate relationship with the infinitely loveable Christ, choose one of these practices and focus on it this week. Offer your practice to the Lord as a gift. Something beautiful will happen for you—guaranteed.

FOURTH WEEK OF LENT: LAETARE SUNDAY

Cultivating Joy

Suggested Scripture Readings

Along with those listed in this section, you may wish to reflect on Philippians 4:8; Matthew 7:1–5; John 16:24, 17:13; Ephesians 3:14–19; Psalm 33:1–5.

Reflection

The Church understands that when we are giving effort to our growth, a foretaste of the result we seek helps us. So today is for cultivating joy and we are invited to live with joy all week. It's a heart-enlivening time, a period of promise, and a hint of the Easter transformation experience we are seeking.

There is a verse in John's Gospel that is often ignored. Jesus is explaining his purpose to his disciples just before the passion: "I have said these things to you so that my joy may be in you, and that your joy may be complete" (15:11).

Joy was what Jesus was about! Do we allow that realization to sink in? Jesus didn't mean joy in some far-off heaven after we suffer our whole lives. Christ intended that, by following him and experiencing him here, we could live joyfully right now in this life.

Wouldn't it be wonderful to live in complete joy? If joy were always present and dependent only on closeness to Jesus Christ, then how might life change? Even pain could not touch the joy of the loving Christ within us. It would be merely another situation from which to learn deeper love. Lesser things, amid this mighty joy, become—well, less!

How can we cultivate Jesus' joy?

First, pray for it. It is Christ's pleasure to give us his joy—but we must be open to receiving it. Asking opens us. Ask for the joy of Christ, the joy of God. It will be poured into you in the exact degree of your openness. It is never God who limits our joy. It is always us.

Second, reflect on what it would have been like to experience the gifts of Jesus: the parents who received their daughter back from death (Luke 8:49–56); the beggar, born blind, who could now see (John 9); Mary Magdalene who first saw the risen Christ (John 20:11–18); the adulteress who's life he saved (John 8:3–11); the possessed man from Gerasa (Luke 8:26–39). You can imagine yourself to be each of these people in turn, letting your delight increase as you "catch" the joy of new life beginning.

Third, each day you can bring pleasure and joy to someone: send flowers, just because; call somebody up and express your appreciation for them; compliment everyone you meet; let your family know, more than usual, how precious they are to you; say "I love you" a lot; be extra kind to a store clerk; or send an unexpected note of good wishes to someone. A week of this is guaranteed to enliven your heart with joy! You'll find the joyful Christ within you.

Practices for the Week

One reason we don't stay joyful is that our will is not yet powerful enough to contain joy when it comes. Our thoughts often erode joy and our will cannot yet control those thoughts. So the empowerment practices for this week are aimed at that immaturity.

Sometimes we engage in conversations that erode the power of our will and obviously kill our joy. One of these is "ain't it awful." You know how it goes: moaning about the government or its participants; wailing about inflation (or recession); finding fault with one group or another; and on and on and on. It can be seductive, this game, because we may agree that things are not as good as they could be. But focusing on the nastiness in life only weakens us.

And joy? It is far away after one of those conversations. So, this week, you may wish to give up all thoughts and words about "ain't it awful."

Another great discipline for empowering our will is to practice not having opinions about others. Practice being a loving, indulgent observer of those around you—rather like the way a parent watches a small child learning to walk. Try staying in touch with the warmth of your own heart and not letting opinions shut down your will.

One more: let go of your attachment to the results of what you do. Attachment is the biggest obstacle to joy. Attachment means feeling as if you *must* have a certain result, or you *must* be a certain way, or happiness cannot come to you. Most of us do plan our activities to get results. How often do we choose to do something only for the pleasure of doing it? Or only as an expression of love, freely given? To let go of any hoped-for result will empower your will.

Fifth Week of Lent

Forgiveness Enlivens Our Hearts

Suggested Scripture Readings

Matthew 18:21–35; Ephesians 4:30—5:2; Luke 7:36–48 (There are puzzles in this story—think about them!); Psalm 130:3–7

Reflection

This week, the two themes we have been following—enlivening the heart and empowering the will—come together. This week's practice is also less optional than the others, if we wish to experience the transformation of Easter's joy and love. This practice is forgiveness.

Everyone knows forgiveness is important, but many people find it difficult. Some misunderstand its nature, others misunderstand its purpose. Forgiveness is not about the perpetrator, not at all. It's not about justifying anyone else's actions. Forgiveness is for ourselves, to free ourselves from the misery of resentments and kept anger. When we forgive, pain is released from our own psyche. Our inner being is livelier and more able to experience joy.

When Jesus spoke about forgiveness (Matthew 18:21–35), he promised Peter a tortuous time if he did not forgive everything and everyone. Jesus was a supreme psychologist. Here the torture will not be imposed from the outside. It comes unavoidably, inside us, with every bit of anger we hang on to, even the justified kind. When we let go of all anger, we choose peace of heart. Then we have an inner environment that supports a loving joyfulness.

Forgiving requires an act of our will, a decision to let go of our anger. This act will use whatever strength our will already has and, in the same instant, will empower our will even more. Then, the decision made, we have only to let go of the negative emotions inside. Letting go also often requires an act of will—this time, it is willingness.

Forgiving also enlivens our heart. It frees the heart from resentment that prevents us from experiencing the love of God for us. You may actually feel your heart dancing in its new freedom—I did. All the energies that I had tied up in being peeved were suddenly at my disposal for loving. That is a lot more enjoyable.

Practices for the Week

Each day this week, spend some quiet time. Pray for awareness of the presence of the all-forgiving Christ. Express your desire to forgive everything that you have ever held against anyone. Then each day, recall one-seventh of your life (if you are forty-nine, recall the first seven years, and so on). Review it to find anything in that period that you have not yet forgiven. In your imagination, take that event or person in your hand and offer it to Christ. Just give it away. See him taking it gently and happily and tucking it into his own heart, where it will be dissolved. Then imagine him giving you a bubble from his heart, full of joy, full of love. Place that bubble in your own heart. Thank him! Then go to the next memory.

This is a happy exercise. Your heart will love it. New power will appear in your will. You will be ready for the intensity and compassion of Holy Week.

HOLY WEEK

We Have Come This Far

Suggested Scripture Readings

All in John's Gospel: 5:11; 14:12–14; 14:15, 21; 14:25–26; 15:7–8; 15:9–11; 15:17; 16:24; 17:13

Reflection

You have come far since Ash Wednesday. You have cooperated with the Spirit within you. And now we stand at the threshold of Holy Week.

It opens with the magnificent ride Jesus took on a donkey's colt into Jerusalem, welcomed with joyful shouts and singing by the people who put their cloaks in the road to honor his passing. The ordinary folk of Jerusalem knew him and were thrilled that he was among them. After all, hadn't he just raised Lazarus from the dead in a nearby town? And now, here he was. What marvel would happen? As we know, what happened was hardly expected on Palm Sunday.

Practices for the Week

So in this, the final week of Lent, you may wish to review your experience of the last five weeks. Take some time to look over your journal and ponder each week. The Christ has been active within you: what is different now? For what change would you like to welcome Jesus anew into the city of your heart? For what new understanding would you like to praise him? For what increase in love would you like to sing to him? Enter these prayers of thanks and praise in your journal.

This is a day for joyful prayer. We also anticipate the passion. Before we jump to Jesus' suffering, death, and resurrection, let's look at three important incidents and teachings that the gospels place during the first Holy Week.

On Monday, you may wish to reflect on one of the most poignant moments in Jesus' ministry, found in Luke 19:41–42. Jesus was entering the city amid praise, but seeing Jerusalem, he wept. He wept over Jerusalem because he saw what it could be, what it needed, and what it actually was.

Have you ever wondered if Jesus would weep over you? Does he see your great potential? Does he know what you need? Does he recognize your limitations and weep. Such love those tears reveal! How would you answer his tears?

On Tuesday, you are invited to consider Matthew 25:14–30, the familiar parable of the "talents" (a talent was a coin). Jesus was telling his followers that he was going away, but he left gifts for them. The question of the parable is, what do we do with those gifts? Perhaps our gifts are money, like the original story. More likely, they are abilities, longings, capacities, and loving desires. Today ask yourself which of the people in Jesus' story you most identify with. Then answer this for yourself and for God: What do I wish to do about what I've discovered?

On Wednesday, you may think about the teaching of Jesus in John 12:24–26. John has placed these words just before the events of Holy Thursday, though his disciples at the time couldn't have understood that connection.

Today, we see that it gives, in part, the meaning of Jesus' willingness to die: so that the fruit desired by the Father in the world might come to fullness. The passage closes with an appeal to the disciple to be like Jesus, for the same reason. Jesus isn't talking only about physical death, but about the willingness of the disciple to give everything of himself to God, so as to bear maximum fruit in our modern world. The questions confronting each of us here are, how much do we cling to how we want our life to be? And how eager are we to give our life over to the purposes of God's love in the world?

When we move to Holy Thursday with that question in our hearts, it can be useful to consider Jesus' words said during the Last Supper in John's Gospel. Chapters 14 to 16 are some of the most beautiful and profound teaching of which we have record. You might want to read these three chapters early on Holy Thursday.

Much of this section is about love or peace or joy or power—all gifts that Jesus says he wants his followers to enjoy. Read to find all these wonderful gifts in this passage. The Master did not want suffering for us (14:1). Write about all comments on joy, love, peace, and power in your journal.

When I consider that all these immense, splendid, desirable qualities of life were promised just before Jesus was arrested, I feel awe. Jesus was so clear. He was thinking so much about his disciples and what he wanted them to understand, even while he was dying. He knew there was much they had yet to grasp, so he promised them the inner Holy Spirit, who would remind them of all his teaching (14:25–26). How could Jesus have been more caring?

How could he have loved us more? All he wanted for us—and was willing to live his whole life, teach and heal, and die too—was love and joy and peace and power. Are we paying enough attention?

THE TRIDUUM

Experiencing the Transformation

Suggested Scripture Readings

Any of the passion or resurrection stories: Matthew 26—28; Luke 22—24; John 18—21

Reflection

Now begin the most sacred three days of the Christian year. We have been reflecting, praying, and practicing for all of Lent to be able to receive great blessings during these three days: Good Friday, Holy Saturday, and Easter. Are you ready?

Good Friday: Let's clear away a stumbling block. Over the years many people have expressed to me that they were worried about themselves because they can't feel mournful on Good Friday. If that's you, be comforted! Jesus didn't do it to make us sorrowful. Remember, he did it for our joy. How can we look at the crucifixion and connect with joy?

First, let's ponder what Meister Eckhart said: Jesus' own experience on the cross was twofold. The outer, physical man was in pain, but the inner man was filled with joy. That is our hint. We honor so deeply the extreme death that Jesus was willing to experience, so we could understand that love is the only thing that matters, and love always brings joy, no matter what it may look like outwardly. He offered this (at the very least) so we can experience our challenges in life without losing our inner awareness of joy.

What else is possible on Good Friday? Gratitude, even for those parts that we don't fully understand. Profound respect for Jesus, so utterly complete in his integrity and his obedience. You may pray for more insights. In still listening, they will be given.

Holy Saturday: Often we get caught up in using Holy Saturday to prepare a lot of food, gifts, Easter eggs, and so on. Maybe you'd like to do something different this year.

If you possibly can, take Holy Saturday as a quiet day—or at least an hour or two. The church is stripped bare and the tabernacle is empty today. If we open to that in our hearts, we find a deep solitude. Nothing big is happening today, and there are no spiritual demands. Be still. Know. Appreciate.

Holy Saturday is an opportunity to recall what your Holy Week has brought you as well. Before Holy Thursday, you may have followed the reflections in this pamphlet. You may have attended special services. Perhaps you went to Mass on Holy Thursday and participated in the washing of feet, as Jesus showed us. On Friday you may have gone to an observance of the Stations of the Cross or some other remembrance. What beauty has this week brought you that you will want to remember always? Have you entered it in your journal?

Easter Sunday: Resurrection is so stupendous—and so familiar—that it's almost impossible to regain our awe over it. Theology has been taught about it, moral conclusions drawn from it, workshops created around it. Most of all, our understanding of Jesus as God can put a great distance between the resurrected Christ and ourselves. Thus we can lose much of Easter's meaning and all of its feeling.

Jesus was also a fully human person. We hear over and over that he struggled as we do, but we neglect the equally vital reality that he laughed and cried, ate and drank, was courteous and surprising—just like the rest of us. So this Easter, how about becoming better acquainted with Jesus as a person you could have had easy conversation with (and can still)?

All the stories show us something fascinating about Jesus: he came to people right where they were. He met a couple walking on a road; he entered a room to be with his closest friends—that's where they were hiding; he met Mary Magdalene in the cemetery garden, where she was mourning. It is the same for us: look for Jesus where you are for that is where he will meet you.

A wonderful opportunity for this experience is in John 21:1–14. Here the risen Jesus is cooking and sharing breakfast on the beach with his disciples. In your loving imagination, you are invited to join them. In fact, you're on the beach with Jesus before the disciples arrive with their big catch of fish—and Peter is soaked because he couldn't wait for the boat to arrive and jumped into the water. It's early yet, barely dawn. Just be there with Jesus, listen to the fish frying, and have a chat before the others arrive.

Isn't it kind of him to cook for everyone?

Aren't you glad you're invited? What else do you feel? Are you happy to see Jesus? Perhaps you'd heard about the crucifixion. Yet here he is, visiting with you as if he'd never left.

Your imagination is a vital factor in your spiritual life. Reflecting imaginatively on Scripture, as we've done during this Lent, is a favorite method of Saint Ignatius. It is one of the best ways to help you feel that Jesus is real and available—as indeed he is. Use it fully on this Easter morning, so that your heart may open to the beauty of the love he always brings. Let it into your being. The love of Jesus Christ is meant for you—and especially on this most happy of happy days!

Easter can indeed be the first day of a transformed life. Here we experience that death—our own physical death and every symbolic death we experience—is always and only a transition to a higher form of life. Let this truth, demonstrated by Jesus, resonate in your heart until

Contributors

David Baldwin
Ashley Beck
Martin Blake
Joanna Bogle
Vivian Boland OP
Richard Brown
Stratford Caldecott
Nick Donelly
Piero Finaldi
Patrick Fleischer
Donal Foley
Marcus Holden
Mark Langham
Amette Ley
Fergal Martin
Barry Midgley
Jennifer Moorcroft
Fiorella Nash
Charlie O'Donnell
Susan Parsons
Helena Scott
Peter Sefton-Williams
Ethel Tolanski
Brendan Walsh
Stephen Wang
Richard Whinder
Eldred Willey
Petroc Willey

you relax a little over any fear of change that you may have. It's a learning process, one that you can consciously begin to integrate today, on Easter, on this beautiful celebration of the permanence and persistence of life itself.

When you feel complete with this reflection, you may wish to invent a couple ways to express your happiness and gratitude for your experience. You could write in your journal. You could share your experience with someone else. You'll be going to Easter Mass, so you can make it part of your Eucharist. You can buy flowers for your Easter dinner table. When you contribute to a special day like this, from your own happy heart, you increase your joy and add to others' delight too.

And finally...

Haven't you had a wonderful Lent?

Please revel in your Easter celebration. Honor the risen Christ and make him part of everything you do today. Welcome him in your thoughts, in your heart. Enjoy his very real presence. Share your love with others. Rejoice in your own new beginnings.

And remember, Easter is the first day of a whole season of celebration. Make it a great one, so your heart-enlivening and will-empowering Lent will bear the greatest possible fruit!